The 5 Keys to Unlock Donor Generosity

for
Anyone Who Wants
to Do More Good!

By Greg Doepke, CAP®, CFP®
with William Summey, Ph.D.

Copyright © 2021 by Aspire to Give LLC.

All rights reserved. Printed in the United States of America. No part of this work may be reproduced or transmitted in any form, or by any means, without the prior written permission of the author.

This publication is designed to provide accurate and authoritative information. The content presented herein, however, is not legal, financialv, or accounting advice, is not to be acted on as such, and may not be current.

If you have questions about anything presented herein as it relates to your legal or financial situation, it is best to contact a trusted professional and seek his or her advice. The author and Aspire to Give® cannot be held responsible for any loss incurred as a result of specific planning decisions made by the reader. For permission for information about permission to reproduce selections from this book, contact *author@aspiretogive.com*.

About Greg Doepke

Greg Doepke is the founder of Aspire to Give® and the architect and author of The Aspirational Philanthropist Learning Series℠, a tailored program developed to unleash the individual human spirit to give generously. Greg serves as the Philanthropist in Residence at Auburn University's Cary Center for the Advancement of Philanthropy and Nonprofit studies. He served on the Board of Directors for the International Association for Advisors in Philanthropy. As a West Point graduate with a passion for servant leadership and over 20 years of credentialed expertise in all facets of financial, estate, legacy, and philanthropic planning, Greg is dedicated to helping each individual recognize and elicit their potential to better themselves, their families, their communities, and our nation.

Greg is married to Suzette, a shining example of a caring, loving heart who is the inspiration for Aspire, the avatar for Aspire to Give®. Suzette is a retired kindergarten teacher who is a shining example of giving, caring, and loving family and friends. Suzette and Greg have two kind, generous daughters, seven thriving grandchildren, and happily reside in Auburn, Alabama.

About William Summey

William Summey, Ph.D., has served as the primary editor for the Aspirational Philanthropist Learning℠ Series and adapted course 1 to this book. William is an adjunct instructor in the College of Theology and Christian Ministry at Belmont University, began his work with philanthropy as managing editor of Paragon Road's *Legacy Arts* magazine, and has worked for over 20 years in the publishing industry.

Dedication

I dedicate this book to all those who love, teach, and serve a cause greater than self to better the lives of others.

Acknowledgments

The onset of COVID and the pandemic served as an imposed, isolating opportunity to survey the philanthropic landscape, research, learn, and record how we — as individuals — might awaken and embrace our inherent nature to give to serve a greater good. The outcome of the opportunity is this book that would not have been possible without the help of others.

Thank you — William Summey and Dayton Cook — for their outstanding team effort and professional skills at editing, designing, and publishing this book. Their insights, organization, and attention to detail have been invaluable.

Thank you — Sid James, Kim Walker, and Mary Elizabeth Fukai — of the Cary Center for the Advancement of Philanthropy and Nonprofit Studies and the Women's Philanthropy Board (WPB) at Auburn University. Their unwavering collaborative support, guidance, and creativity have been instrumental in advancing philanthropy through donor education.

As a resource for the last twenty years, the professional staff at the Community Foundation for a Greater Richmond has openly shared their dedicated professional expertise, experience, and initiatives to advance philanthropy. They are the gold standard for caring, sharing, and serving their greater community. Thank you, Richmond!

Above all, I am deeply grateful to my wife, Suzette, for her continuing love, support, and encouragement. Suzette is the inspiration for Aspire, the avatar and symbol of the giving heart in this book and throughout The Aspirational Philanthropist Learning Series℠. She serves as a giving, loving role model for her family, friends, and all who know her.

Let's do some good!

Greg Doepke

Oct 26, 2021

Table of Contents

Preface 1

Part I. Re-framing Philanthropic Conversations

Chapter 1: Embrace a Different Outlook 7
Chapter 2: Tap Your Donor Roots 12
Chapter 3: Engage Your Circles of Influence 17

Part II. The 5 Keys

Chapter 4: Key #1: Inquire to Learn 23
Chapter 5: Key #2: Appreciate Your Wheelhouse Gifts ... 30
Chapter 6: Key #3: Understand Your Life Journey
  Phase 1 Accumulation 36
Chapter 7: Key #3: Understand Your Life Journey
  Phase 2 Opportunity 41
Chapter 8: Key #3: Understand Your Life Journey
  Phase 3 Distribution 45
Chapter 9: Key #4: Engage in
  Meaningful Conversations 49
Chapter 10: Key #5: Follow the Donor's Roadmap ... 54

Part III. Leverage the 5 Keys for a Brighter Future

Chapter 11: Recap the Basics 62
The Aspirational Philanthropist Learning Series℠ ... 65

Part IV. Donor-Outlook Enrichment Readings

Enrichment Reading A: Advancing Philanthropy
  Through the Eyes & Heart of the Donor 69
Enrichment Reading B: Why Do You Get up
  in the Morning? 72
Enrichment Reading C: The 5 Pillars of
  Hometown Philanthropy 75
Enrichment Reading D: The 7 Essential Questions
  for Smart Giving 78

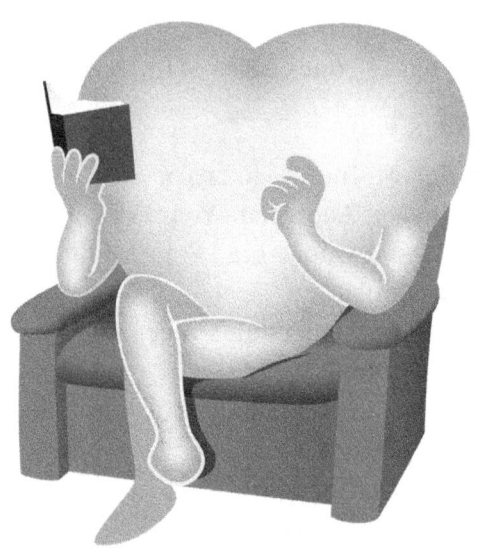

Preface

Welcome to The *5 Keys to Unlock Donor Generosity*! I am Greg Doepke, and I am honored to serve as the Philanthropist in Residence at Auburn University's Cary Center for the Advancement of Philanthropy and Nonprofit Studies. I am also the architect, author, and instructor for The Aspirational Philanthropist Learning Series℠, courses that empower donors to be the best stewards of their resources as they strive to do good for their families and their favorite causes. This groundbreaking series was developed to advance philanthropy and is a joint initiative of the Cary Center and Aspire to Give®. On behalf of the Cary Center and Aspire to Give®, thank you for investing your time in this book, which is based on the content of Course 1 of the learning series.

The Aspirational Philanthropist Learning Series℠ is a 4-course program that guides anyone who wants to do more for their family and meaningful causes. The series consists of four sequential courses: Donor Fundamentals, Donor Discovery, Donor Design, and Donor Legacy.

This book embodies the content of the Donor Fundamentals course. It serves to provide anyone who wants to do more for their family and causes with a basic understanding of what it means to be an effective donor. It can serve as a stand-alone course or as the foundation and entry to the tailored and more personal courses of Donor Discovery, Donor Design, and Donor Legacy. These last three courses of the learning series allow the individual to take  a deeper dive and tailor their own giving strategy to both family and causes.

The four unique qualities of this program include the following — all of which will be developed further throughout the book.

1. A change to a donor-outlook perspective (Chapter 1).
2. A strengths-based, life-giving approach of appreciative inquiry (Chapter 4).
3. The emphasis on donor-outlook questioning tools and techniques (Chapters 4-8).
4. The Series' educational design breaks down two sets of silos that have restricted donor effectiveness. These silos are:
   1. Giving to family vs. giving to outreach
   2. Donor conversations with nonprofits vs. donor advisors

Breaking down these silos improves donor effectiveness with more meaningful conversations and better decision-making.

Someone commented to me how innovative this approach to donors is. Thinking about the term innovative caused me to pause. If we take a step back and look at our surroundings, innovations continue to improve almost every aspect of our lives. Examples abound everywhere!

During COVID, innovation was at the forefront of rapid vaccine development and our ability to adapt to the pandemic's health challenges. Yet, despite ongoing innovation in all sectors of our society, we face numerous challenges, such as homelessness, inequality, divisiveness, environmental issues, and many others.

There is no doubt — now is the time! There is an overwhelming need to innovate in philanthropy to meet our societal challenges. We need to advance philanthropy through innovation.

I have to agree with the word innovation. The Aspirational Philanthropist Learning Series℠ advances philanthropy with a different way of thinking. This different approach is at the core of this book. It embraces a paradigm shift in perspective with a bottom-up, grassroots outlook that empowers each of us as aspiring philanthropists. This philosophy views philanthropy through the heart and the eyes of the donor. It equips the individual donor with a positive, life-giving, questioning approach and the knowledge, tools, roadmap, and resources to better their families and meaningful causes. This point of view shares many similarities to other cultural movements, such as effective altruism, which seeks to accomplish the most good.

The Seven Beliefs of Donor-outlook Philanthropy

So, what does this new perspective look like? To help you visualize it better, these are the seven basic beliefs of this movement called Donor-outlook Philanthropy. Many of these will be discussed in greater detail throughout the book as part of a roadmap for you, but it is important to grasp how this perspective is different than other approaches.

1. Donor-outlook philanthropy is about the perspective. It starts from the viewpoint of the individual doing good for both the family and important causes. Donor-outlook philanthropy is about each of us. It recognizes and emphasizes our inherent goodness and the gifts we each carry with us, many of which we don't even realize we possess.

2. Donor-outlook philanthropy is grassroots. Giving comes from the depths of our souls. Giving is important to our well-being, as many of the physical needs are to us, such as food, air, and water. To give to something greater than self is embedded in our DNA and brings meaning and purpose to life.

3. Donor-outlook philanthropy is about unleashing our four inherent and accumulated gifts. Like many things in life, a giving heart and spirit needs to be recognized, awakened, and energized to learn to use the four gifts we each carry with us to make a positive impact in the world.

4. Donor-outlook philanthropy is appreciative, life-giving, and strengths-based. We all like to be valued, appreciated, and believe that we gain meaning from our lives by utilizing our individual experience,

talents, and resources for the benefit of others or causes greater than self.

5. Donor-outlook philanthropy recognizes the value of individual diversity and inclusion. With the appreciation of each individual's uniqueness, perspectives, and strengths, the power of diversity to reach common aligned goals can be unleashed for the common good.

6. Donor-outlook philanthropy embraces servant leadership. Whether it be the individual or a diverse and inclusive group of stakeholders working towards a common goal, leaders must serve others first through the appreciation and unleashing of individual goodness and gifts for giving.

7. Donor-outlook philanthropy can leverage technology to magnify impact. The unleashing of each individual's human potential through technology will result in socially innovative solutions to our many societal challenges.

It is our sincere hope, dream, and passion that this book may empower each of you— as aspiring philanthropists— to make a difference. Thank you for embarking on this learning journey!

Part I. Re-framing Philanthropic Conversations

CHAPTER 1

Embrace a Different Outlook

In my previous career helping clients financially prepare for, transition into, and enjoy retirement, I learned and received far more from my clients than all the knowledge and expertise I shared with them. Over more than 20 years, I came to know my clients as caring, loving people who wanted to make a difference with their families and communities.

As my career evolved into philanthropy, I began to question the directional flow of knowledge, advice, and guidance— both financial and philanthropic conversations were almost always one way. The advice was downhill from the nonprofit or the professional advisor to the donor. Yet, my clients always wanted to know more, were eager to learn, and aspired to become better philanthropists. I also began to see the challenges that my clients had to overcome. As aspiring philanthropists, my clients had to engage with, learn from, and process the advice and guidance from nonprofits and many professional advisors, such as myself, their CPA, lawyer, and others. I recognized that a key to learning is asking good questions. And to ask good questions, you must be familiar with fundamental concepts and terminology.

Then I began to ask questions. I started digging deeper and researching resources where individual donors could learn to care for their families and serve their meaningful causes.

Of course, there are plenty of financial literacy programs. This series is not another one of those financial programs. What I looked for was a course or program to learn to be a more effective donor. I assumed that if we can help donors become better for their families and favorite charities by asking intentional, well-structured questions, we can unleash a storm of human goodness and potential! I wanted to help donors discover, value, and apply their strengths. After all, it is by asking the right questions that we learn, grow, become, and better. What I found is that there are very few learning programs for individual donors.

In most areas of learning, there are multiple choices and options. Education is much like the grocery store's shelves of different brands and varieties of choices available to you — except for donor-outlook philanthropy education. There are over 255 academic programs that provide philanthropy education; however, these programs are almost exclusively dedicated to the top-down approach, addressing nonprofits, fundraising, board governance, and so on. Fill in the blanks. There are very few learning programs, anywhere, for the individual donor! So, there is a significant need for donor-outlook philanthropy programs where the individual learns to do more for both family and their causes.

From a donor's perspective, I also started asking questions about these separate worlds of nonprofits and professional advisors, such as:

1. Why are there separate worlds or silos of nonprofit and professional advisors? How might we integrate them to be easier for the individual donor? Where do we start?
2. With all the many online or group programs available to learn everything from baking cakes to becoming fluent in a foreign language, why is there a lack of programs that teach individual donors how to better their families and their favorite nonprofits? How can we help individual donors become better philanthropists and make a greater impact?

These questions naturally led to two more:

3. What if there were a program or series that bridges the worlds of nonprofits and professional advisors that originates at the grassroots level from the donor's perspective?
4. What if there were courses that provided a donor roadmap — an educational learning process that serves to bridge these worlds and empowers donors to ask better questions?

In a donor-outlook approach, instead of the donor being an object of guidance, advice, and solicitations, the schooled donor becomes more aware, knowledgeable, and capable of effective questioning, resulting in better giving decisions.

There are significant benefits to this donor-outlook approach.

1. The individual donor would be equipped with the language, knowledge, philanthropic tools, and a step-by-step roadmap to foster better questions and decisions for family and community.
2. The learning series fosters effective and meaningful conversations with family members.

3. The worlds of donors, nonprofits, and professional advisors are integrated at the donor level. There is a transformational paradigm shift in perspective and action. Knowledgeable and empowered donors lead and foster collaborative partnering with nonprofits and professional advisors instead of being targeted objects of advice and solicitation.

4. With donors armed with terminology, the know-how, and effective questions, it "raises the bar" on nonprofit guidance and professional advice. Nonprofit professionals and professional advisors will be challenged to become better in their roles as donors become more knowledgeable, confident, and capable.

5. The series fosters trust and caring amongst donors, nonprofits, and professional advisors.

6. The series improves the effectiveness of conversations between donors and their advisors.

7. The different perspective spurs the development in new books, courses, and series that focus on donor-outlook philanthropy.

8. The donor-outlook process integrates both the emotional and rational aspects of giving, providing practical considerations for caring and impactful giving decisions for family and causes.

9. The positive, life-giving, appreciative mindset baked into the learning process inspires an effective approach to overcome local community challenges with the "Appreciative Stakeholder Learning Process."

In summary, to advance philanthropy, this grassroots learning series leverages the major shift in perspective to donor-outlook that leverages professional and nonprofit guidance with the power of an enlightened, more effective donor. The role of the donor flips from being the object of guidance, advice, and solicitation to an empowered, informed, questioning donor. In addition, the donor gains more meaning with wiser, intentional giving to both family and outreach.

If you take a step back and take a higher 10,000-foot viewpoint of the societal challenges we face, we have a lot of good we can do. Despite the history of pouring gobs of money into societal challenges in a top-down flow from the mega-affluent, large institutions, foundations, and government, this aspirational philanthropist perspective takes a different approach. This approach teaches and equips the individual donor with the power to make a difference. The donor jumps in the driver's seat with the knowledge, tools, and roadmap to more effective, impactful decisions for their families and their causes.

There is an axiom, "A rising tide lifts all boats." This new perspective will have the power to lift so many boats– enabling each individual to better their families, engage more fully with nonprofits and fundraising, and raise the bar on professional advisor caring and competence standards.

Another familiar axiom we have all heard is "Knowledge Is Power." If we each — as aspiring philanthropists — learn more on how to better our families and the world, then we can — individually and collectively — be that rising tide, that rising power; that lifts all boats.

CHAPTER 2

Tap Your Donor Roots

Let's talk about the aspiration to give. I join with those who argue that it is an essential characteristic of human existence to give part of oneself that will outlast your life here on earth. This concept is that of self-transcendence. Let me share with you three psychologists who were significant contributors to this concept of self-transcendence.

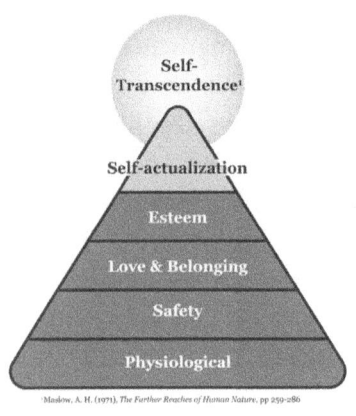

Maslow, A. H. (1971), *The Farther Reaches of Human Nature*, pp 259-286

Abraham Maslow developed his hierarchy of needs that you may have studied in school. His pyramid-shaped hierarchy starts at the base with our basic needs: physiological, safety, love, belonging, and esteem needs.

At the top of the triangle is self-actualization. But later, Maslow augmented his hierarchy to include self-transcendence and placed it above the triangle itself. Maslow's book, *The Farther Reaches of Human Nature*, was published by his wife after his death in 1971. In this work, Dr. Maslow introduces his theory of meta motivation, which he attributes to the concept of self-transcendence or serving something greater than yourself. We transcend ourselves to reach out beyond ourselves in a lasting way.

Another psychologist of note is Dr. Viktor Frankl. Dr. Frankl was a World War II Holocaust survivor, having survived the horrors of Auschwitz. Based on his experience in Auschwitz, Dr. Frankl wrote *Man's Search for Meaning* and subsequently was the founder of logotherapy, a mode of psychology based on our motivation to search for meaning in our lives. This concept is clarified in Dr. Frankl's book *The Will to Meaning: Foundations and Applications of Logotherapy*. Dr. Frankl added to this discussion about self-transcendence and talked about it as part of the human will, an intentional choice.

Dr. Erik H. Erikson is a well-known psychologist widely recognized for his contribution to understanding the stages of human development. In his book, *The Life Cycle Completed*, Dr. Erikson addresses the critical stages of psychological development. His eighth stage includes the struggle of integrity vs. despair as one reflects on life's accomplishments. Joan Erikson introduced the ninth stage of development that is more encompassing and points toward self-transcendence.

Countless others have built on this research that points to the understanding that we seek to become better and strive to be the best version of ourselves that we can be! That involves giving back and investing in others in a way that transcends ourselves. There is a need for self-transcendence that, at its highest level, shows how we need to serve causes that are greater than ourselves. You could say it is in our DNA to give and invest in others. It is who we are, and that is what we are supposed to do. The more we can help and serve others or a cause greater than self, the more meaning we gain in our lives.

Aspire and You

I have created a guide for this learning approach. Aspire is the avatar or the symbol of your giving heart, your inherent desire to serve your family and give to causes. Aspire will serve throughout this book as a reminder that you have to lead with your heart. You should always lead with your heart when dealing with your family and those passions and causes that are important to you. To help introduce my followers to Aspire, I created the following introduction from Aspire's point of view.

Introducing Aspire

There is much to think about when it comes to giving—when it's time to travel on the road to smart, intentional giving—some may find it best to turn to a trusted guide for help along the way. At Aspire to Give®, it is part of our mission to educate and equip generous people with the knowledge and tools to give wisely so they can give because they feel they must give.

To help you as a giving heart expand your understanding of what your personal giving journey could be, we'd like to introduce you to Aspire—a trusted guide in her own right. Aspire is the very being of a giving heart.

Without further ado, meet Aspire!

Hi! I'm Aspire. I am your giving heart. Like you, I love to give to others—and it's something I have always done. But I am now at a point in my life where I have the opportunity to do more! I have learned much on my journey thus far and as I transition into a new stage of life, I realize giving sounds so easy, but can be complicated.

As a caring heart—like you—I want my giving to my family and to causes that are important to me to be well thought out, special to me, beneficial for others, and meaningful. Even though I have been giving my whole life, I know I can do better—and I want to share some tools and tips I have picked up along my own giving journey so far.

You know that feeling you get when you do something kind, when you give—even the smallest thing—to someone, to something other than yourself? It's a good feeling—a warm, fuzzy feeling. And it's the added bonus when you give! Giving isn't about you—it's about others. It's about lending a helping hand. It's about working together to improve something. It's about shared experiences and bringing more people together with common goals to do social good.

Giving is understanding the emotional pull—your heart—to invest in something that's important to you and acknowledging you must engage the pragmatic side of yourself—your head—to do so in a smart, effective way. We can number that tip #1—listen to your giving heart and engage your thinking head—when it comes to mapping out your giving plan. ☺

Since I'm feeling generous, I'll go ahead and share tip #2—think outside the box. Sometimes when we think of giving, we think of only one or two ways to give like a charitable donation or volunteering—but, there are many ways to give.

Like you, it is my goal to be a better person. Together we can map out and navigate the best route to get us to the destination of becoming the best version of ourselves for our family and causes. Along the way we will discover our passion, imagine a future, devise a plan and see how it can be put into action. Sounds fun, right?

Join me on this giving adventure that will lead to impactful and meaningful life moments!

With the Spirit of Giving,
Love,
Aspire

I want you to understand that this book and this life-giving approach to donor-outlook philanthropy are about appreciating and celebrating — you! It is all about fostering your family, your inclination to give, and your humanity.

Our celebration of you and the appreciation of all that you are is an uplifting, strengths-based, and life-giving approach. It focuses on your inherent goodness to do good and your aspiration to give and transcend self.

We join with you in celebrating what you care about: your family, your unique story, your gifts, your passions, your strengths, what you love, what you enjoy, and what is meaningful to you. This approach is all about appreciating and celebrating you to become the best donor you can be!

CHAPTER 3

Engage Your Circles of Influence

This book and donor-outlook approach to philanthropy are about change. It is about equipping you to change the future of your family and those causes you care about. To begin with, let's examine where you are now. That is what this book is all about.

Oprah Winfrey once said, "For every one of us who achieves success, it is because there's somebody there to show the way." Taking Oprah's quote a step further, usually, there is more than just one person to show us the way. We all need help finding our way to becoming better donors. This help will be in the form of confidants, family members, guides, coaches, and advisors.

I talk about all of those who are part of our learning process and giving as our circles of influence. There are four primary circles of influence.

1. Your inner circle
2. Your advisory circle
3. Your learning circle
4. Your beneficiary circle

This chapter will focus on your first two circles of influence — the inner circle and the advisory circle.

The Inner Circle

I like to explain that your inner and advisory circle is much like your family gathered around the table at Thanksgiving for the harvest feast. You are sitting at the head of the table, and you are leading.
You are carving the turkey, but you are responsive to the wants and needs of those around the table as to the type of turkey and the amount they want.

Now, imagine that instead of a Thanksgiving dinner table, you are sitting at the head of the Donor's Table as shown below.

You engagingly lead your inner circle. They are the ones at the table that are closest to you. You seek input, guidance, and feedback from those around your table as to your future hopes, dreams, and goals to impact others. As Aspire reminds us, you are always leading with your heart.

Your inner circle includes, first and foremost, your significant other. Your significant other is someone close to you who is trusted and serves as your confidential sounding board for thoughts, feedback, and insights. This person is always at your right-hand side during the entire giving journey and is usually the first one you confide in regarding your giving. For some, this will be their spouse. For others, it will be a dear friend or a parent. Others will have two significant others, with each serving a distinct role.

Your inner circle should always include your elders, which I describe as members of the previous generation. In most cases, your elders are your parents, aunts, uncles, mentors, or someone else close to you — but an older generation with more life experiences. They serve as essential older guides for you in family-related matters.

The last members of your inner circle are life-learners. Life-learners are typically one generation younger than you. They may be your children or others you love and care for. You may serve as their life guides and show them the ropes of life. You pass on to them your life chapters and wisdom. But you will realize how much you can learn from life-learners as well. Their unique strengths, perspectives, and environment can inspire you as to possibilities for the future. It is essential to keep an open mind with your life-learners to listen and learn from them!

So, in reviewing the inner circle members, you should try to include three generations and a broad age spectrum—you have life-learners as the younger generation, your significant other in the donor's generation, and elders as the older generation.

Your Advisory Circle

At the opposite end of the table – those furthest from you – are your advisory circle members. You will seek out and engage confidants, guides, coaches, and advisors for their counsel and input to ensure you follow your moral compass to design and implement your strategy to achieve your giving goals. These people help guide and serve you. You might think of these as not around your Thanksgiving table but as members of a special business meeting of which you are the chair.

Think of each member of the advisory circle as filling a distinct role. The advisory circle is at your table to provide you with their trusted advice and guidance. Still, you will need to engage them for their unique professional input, expertise, and counsel. Remember that you are the team leader of this circle as well.

An important part of this process is uncovering and clarifying what causes are meaningful to you. This process includes affirming categories of causes and then narrowing your focus to identify further and vet aligned nonprofits and other organizations that advance your causes. Associated with these nonprofits and other organizations are their employed professionals whose purpose is to engage you, cultivate a relationship, and solicit you for your support to meet their specific mission. These nonprofit professionals are part of your advisory circle.

There are also professional advisors. Typically, these members may be your CPA, CFP®, financial or investment advisor, insurance professional, and lawyer. You may even access a chartered advisor in philanthropy (CAP®). These professional advisors are typically experts in their field. Still, many times professional advisors are not comfortable nor capable of discussing philanthropy with you.

For some, this book may be enough to serve as a guide for your giving strategy. Others may have a donor coach to provide more tailored guidance. For others, a pastor may serve in this role. This role is often a non-family mentor who answers questions, serves as a sounding board, and will help connect you with other resources you may need.

The most trusted member of your advisory circle often becomes an additional member of your inner circle. This person becomes the one who most closely helps serve as a guide for designing and implementing your giving strategy.

In this chapter, you learned about the four circles of influence – inner, advisory, learning, and beneficiary. You understand that you are the team leader of your circles. Your inner circle is made of those closest to you. Your advisory circle provides trusted guidance and advice. By applying philanthropic inquiry to ask sound questions, you will learn to engage your inner and advisory circles so that you, as the donor, will make intelligent and effective giving decisions.

Part II. The 5 Keys

Now, we get into the core of this book: the five keys to effective giving. If we are looking to become the best philanthropist we can be, we need to have a method to approach our giving in a smarter, effective way. We will need a tool to frame and structure our given strategy, reveal answers, explore possibilities, and ensure wise, effective decision-making. For framing our giving strategy, we need to ensure it includes all the various topics of our personal and outreach giving integrated into one approach to help us stay on target.

CHAPTER 4

Key #1: Inquire to Learn

Key #1 to effective giving: the proven application of inquiry or asking questions. Why are questions important? There are so many life situations in which we find ourselves saying: "I wish I knew the right questions to ask!" Have you ever gone to the doctor for an annual checkup, or taken your child, only to remember after the visit questions you should have asked? So, it is with donor-outlook philanthropy. As we learn about effective giving, we will need to know the right questions to ask to reveal answers, learn insights, and develop as a better version of ourselves. Thus, I will plant the seeds of inquiry throughout the remainder of this book. At the end of each chapter, I will include several questions for your consideration that you can use as a basis for formulating your own questions. I encourage you to review these questions in light of your own situation and then craft your own questions that reflect your personal aspiration to give.

Questions are also foundational for innovation. At its root, the Socratic method of asking questions has always been the fuel that drives innovation and advances humankind. If we narrow down the general concept of inquiry, or questioning, to philanthropy, we have a method of philanthropic inquiry (PI). If we target philanthropic inquiry from the outlook of the donor, we have a powerful tool. This tailored philanthropic questioning from the donor's perspective is called donor-outlook questioning (DOQ) for short. We have tailored the broad Socratic method of asking questions to the philanthropic sector and further tapered the approach to asking questions by you, the donor, the aspiring philanthropist. We now have DOQ in our toolkit!

There are many benefits of using DOQ. We can use DOQ to engage others gently, reveal answers and possibilities, and discover new strategies and options. These questions will help you think through your comprehensive giving strategy, engage your family and advisors in better conversations, vet potential beneficiaries, gift your treasure, and open new possibilities. You will target clarity, disclosure, engagement, options, understanding, and decisions with DOQ to cover all the bases.

For this chapter, we will apply one method of DOQ. (I introduce others in future books.) In this chapter, we will review asking seven questions to frame and structure your overall giving plan. We ask these questions to ensure we cover all the bases, don't miss anything, and that our strategy is comprehensive and integrated. We ask seven questions in the right way to elicit answers. The intentional use of seven questions to frame our giving ensures options and comprehensive decisions are well thought out. It helps us make sound financial giving decisions by avoiding financial and tax pitfalls and assures an integrated and well-designed giving strategy.

Let's dive right in and look at how the DOQ method of asking seven questions is used to frame and structure our overall giving strategy. This Socratic approach of asking appreciative, mostly open-ended questions of yourself, your significant other, and other members of your inner circle will be highly beneficial. Assessing your inner circle members' circumstances and seeking their input will enable you to tailor your strategy for greater personal meaning and impact. The seven questions can be categorized into either "giving heart" dominant questions that are emotional and feeling questions or "thinking head" rational and logical questions.

The Giving Heart Questions

The giving heart dominant questions are:

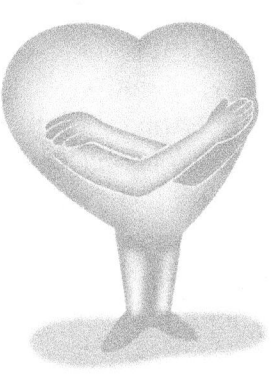

1. Why do you give?
2. Who do you give to?
3. Where do you give?

The most important giving heart question is the why question: why do you give? I call it the big why. I think this question is 100% emotional, passion-driven, and the inspiration for your generosity. It serves as a springboard to the other six questions.

The next question is a logical next step: who do you give to? This question is answered on two levels. The first level is a broader topic or focus area. In the philanthropy sector, this also may be called a field of interest. The second level is much more specific. It is the nonprofit or organization that benefits from your generosity. You should match the focus or field of interest with your passion. It could focus on children's education, the homeless, the environment, financial literacy, veterans, or countless other causes.

Once you have identified the who, the next step is to answer the geographic question: where do I give? Do you want to give locally, regionally, or internationally? Many times, there are why reasons attached to these locations, so it may be helpful to ask further questions, like these: What is your motivation for giving in these geographic areas? For example, you love your hometown, and that is where you want to give your gifts. Or perhaps it was that you lived overseas as a child and saw the poverty of a third-world country. That may be the motivation for your passion for giving internationally.

Whatever the reason, it is vital to understand where you want to give because there are trade-offs in giving your gifts, depending on the location. For example, if you go on a mission trip to a third-world country, you should understand the trade-off between your time and the cost of going on the trip. If you conclude that it makes sense and you are passionate about international giving, move forward.

As you can see, even as we move through these heart-level questions, the need arises to use your thinking head as you zero in on potential beneficiaries of your generosity.

For example, let's say the definite answer to your who question is women's financial education, especially for those women that are divorced or widowed. You have also determined that your where is your hometown. From that point, you can now zero in on the specific organizations in your hometown that have the aligned mission of financial and philanthropic literacy for women.

How do you select the organizations you would like to support? Part of our donor responsibility for effective and impactful giving is to research and clearly understand that the organization is a good match for you. You want to make sure the receiving beneficiary organization of your generosity is a sound steward, and they are making a significant and meaningful impact.

The Thinking Head Questions

Let's turn our attention to the thinking head questions. In many instances, the head-dominant questions are the rational and logical questions asked of your inner and advisory circles as you seek out the targeted guidance of professional advisors and nonprofit professionals. These head-dominant questions are:

1. How do I give?
2. What do I give?
3. When do I give?
4. How much do I give?

How do I give? This question has two levels. On a conceptual level, it refers to your identified positives. When I refer to your positives, I refer that you give from your strengths, and you feel joy and meaning and satisfaction from your giving. It is essential to focus on how your strengths can be meaningful and impactful to you. On a financial level, how you give your financial assets can make a big difference! The gifting of your treasure is concrete, relatable, and easy to understand. For example, you could ask DOQ questions: How might I give family or charity-appreciated property? What if I could benefit my children, give more, and avoid the taxes?

What should I give? Once again, we apply DOQ to see what makes the most sense for us, gives us the most meaning, and makes the intended significant impact. Do I give my talents, time, treasure, or help with connecting people and organizations (trust)? If we look at my financial assets, do I give cash, stocks, bonds, real estate, collections of all kinds, privately held stock, or make in-kind donations?

All of these are part of "treasure" that may be gifted is just a matter of what makes the most emotional and rational sense for ourselves, our family, and the outreach beneficiaries of our generosity.

When should I give? When do you give on your life journey? While living, at death, or both? Should you give before or after you sell a business, real estate, or investments? What about retirement or at a certain age? A lot is dependent on your life journey.

How much should I give? How much do you give of each of the gifts? The answer to the giving of talents and trust is easy — it is always 100%. But there is a caveat! You need to recognize and understand your talents and trust as a strength that brings meaning to you. Since time and treasure are measurable and limited, it comes down to calculating the amount of each. How do you allocate amongst family financial support your financial outreach?

So, there you have the DOQ method of asking seven questions, divided into giving-heart and thinking-head categories. The most important question is why? First and foremost, this question must be answered on the emotional level — from the heart — before you consider the other six questions. Then you have the who? on the focus or field of interest level. Then you answer the Where? geographically. This question, in turn, is followed by the targeted organization who? — those organizations to be researched and adequately vetted. Those are the three questions of the giving heart.

Then you have the four head-dominant questions. With your significant other and donor coach at your side, you should seek out the guidance and input from nonprofit professionals and professional advisors to answer the questions of how to give? what to give? when to give? how much to give?

More Questions to Ponder

1. What is your motivation to give to your favorite nonprofit?
2. As you reflect on your current giving, what brings you the most joy and meaning?
3. Who are your trusted members of your inner and advisory circles?

CHAPTER 5

Key #2: Appreciate Your Wheelhouse Gifts

Let's take a closer look at this key and what we mean by giving wheelhouse. Your giving wheelhouse is all that you are and all you carry with you from which you can choose to give. If you think about it, we are each carrying with us a satchel stocked with tools that are resources from which we can give. And, as you learned in chapter 2, it is in our DNA to give – it is what we were born to do. These assets that you carry with you are all-inclusive. In economic terms, these different assets are referred to as our human capital (our talents), our financial capital (our treasure or money), and our social capital, which also may be referred to as trusted relationships or "trusted ties." We also carry the time — the little moments we have on our short time on earth. These moments are our time capital. Each of us has a tremendous potential to do good with our gifts. We each can make a difference – in our way. To keep the terms simple, for the remainder of this book, I'll simply refer to your giving wheelhouse as a composite collection of strengths in terms of your time, talents, treasure, and trust.

Time is what we all have, and it is a great equalizer. We all have 60 minutes per hour, 24 hours a day, seven days a week, 365 days a year. We don't know how many years we will live, so we should feel fortunate and blessed to have this time. It is our most precious resource. We can choose to either spend our time or invest our time. Since our time is limited, we need to understand the vital importance of structuring our time. Because our time is such a critical concept, we will look more closely at the spending or investing of our time in the next chapter.

The second component of your giving wheelhouse is in the form of human capital. It is simply referred to as your talents. We typically think of talents in terms of our inherent nature: our inborn personality and natural skills. You may be analytical, good at solving math problems, writing essays, or dealing with people. We are born with specific traits, and it is part of who we are. Your talents are also derived from your education. That includes life-skills education, beliefs, and values instilled and modeled by parents and formal, informal, life skills education, and career skills training. Many people also have personal talents such as playing an instrument, artistry, or woodworking. Still, another category of talents is the chapters learned in the school of hard knocks and the life chapters from your family, career, or business. Situations in life may not always be good, but you've learned from those mistakes.

The third component in our giving wheelhouse is our treasure or financial capital. Treasure is typically our financial life, including our money, income, savings, investments, and other financial assets. Or we may be a business owner or have a professional practice, in which case we have value in our business. Other kinds of money are in-kind resources, which are additional items that have financial value. An example would be inventory in a business that  could be contributed to nonprofit community work. For example, let's say you own a building supply company. An in-kind donation of property would be donating lumber to rebuild homes after a devastating tornado. We also may have similar in-kind personal resources, such as donating an old car or some rarely worn clothes sitting in our closets.

The last component in our giving wheelhouse is our social capital, our trusted relationships. Trusted relationships are  often overlooked! We routinely hear about our time, talent, and treasure but hear very little about the value of our trusted relationships as a gift in our wheelhouse. We develop trusted relationships over time. Whether they be personal, family, social, community, or professional, we all have someone to call on at a time of need. Awaken to those relationships that are part of your life. Nurture and care for them. With trusted relationships, you will bring a whole new dimension to all the good you can do! You can share trusted relationships by connecting people through mentoring, coaching, teaching, and sharing your time with family, friends, and those in need. People want and need to give, so recognizing this particular gift and extending your trust can bring you a whole new level of impact, satisfaction, and personal meaning.

Our gifts are unique to each of us (and that's OK!). Think of differences in each individual's wheelhouse gifts as another form of diversity.

Some people have very little time because they are busy with family, school, career, or caring for a loved one. Other people may have a lot of time, such as those who are retired or have flexibility in their schedules.

Everyone has talents of some kind. Many people have hidden talents that are not obvious. They may not be formally educated, but they have hidden talents because of their life journey and experiences. It's vital to understand that everybody has hidden talents. It's just a matter of identifying, understanding, and applying the unique, life-giving, positive, strengths-based talents that each person has. It is essential to understand perspectives or attitudes that may be hidden and benefit others. Some people have many talents, formal education, and professional development in multiple careers. They have developed an inventory of many talents that they developed over their lifetime. The amount we have of each of these gifts is unique for each of us. It is not a matter of good or bad. It is just different, and they can all be used to do good.

Consider your treasure. You may not have much money. You may be very poor in income, financial savings, or net worth. Others may have a lot of money.

Lastly, consider trust or our relationships. Some of us are not very social. You may be introverted with a few relationships. You are not on social media and are comfortable keeping a few relationships. That's OK. It's just unique to you. Or there may be some who have many relationships and are the proverbial social butterfly. They have many personal, professional, and social relationships and are very active on social media. You must understand where you are on the spectrum with your trusted relationships and that no matter what, you can tap and share with these trusted relationships. It is essential to recognize that people want and need to give. Sometimes, it is just a matter of asking!

This donor-outlook recognizes and appreciates your uniqueness and all that you are with your potential gifts of time, human, financial, and social capital – your time, talents, treasure, and trust. It also recognizes that differences in others are also to be appreciated and celebrated.

No matter your life position, no matter your economic situation, you are carrying around with you your time, talents, treasure, and trust, no matter where you are in life. And so is everyone else! This combination is your giving wheelhouse, and it is a potential gold mine to unearth and do good.

This book is all about celebrating and appreciating you, as well as each individual, no matter what your background or situation. First and foremost, it appreciates your unique wheelhouse. Recognize that others have their special wheelhouse. No two wheelhouses are the same, and that is good!

In the next chapter, we will learn more about how we acquire and give these wheelhouse gifts. We will learn their role in our lives as we look at the life journey of aspirational giving.

More Questions to Ponder

1. When was the last time you tapped your trusted connections to help a nonprofit organization?
2. Which of your four wheelhouse gifts is your greatest strength?
3. What are the primary wheelhouse strengths of one of your inner circle members?

CHAPTER 6

Key #3: Understand Your Life Journey

Phase 1 Accumulation

Thus far, you have been introduced to the roots of your giving, your four circles of influence, and key #1 - the use of questions to reveal and discover. We've covered key #2—your giving wheelhouse — which includes the four gifts we all carry with us. These four gifts are our time, talents, treasure, and the most overlooked gift we each have — trust — our trusted relationships.

For key #3, we will talk about our life journey. Because of the amount of material, this key is divided into three chapters. This first chapter will cover Phase 1 Accumulation, the next chapter will cover Phase 2 Opportunity, and Chapter 8 will cover Phase 3 Distribution.

First, let's discuss how we are all on a journey, the road of life, from our birth to our death. From an individual, donor-outlook perspective, I have coined this the Life Journey of Aspirational Giving. From a 10,000-foot level, let's take a look at this typical life journey we are all traveling. We will then dig deeper and look more closely at the stages of the journey. In particular, we will look at the gifts in the giving wheelhouse during this life journey, recognize their importance, and see how the wheelhouse of gifts changes over time.

In my previous professional practice helping people prepare for, transition into, and navigate a successful retirement, I commonly used a bell curve to represent a graphical depiction of the accumulation of financial savings and their distribution over time. Several years ago, I read *The Longevity Economic: Unlocking the World's Fastest-Growing, Most Misunderstood Market* by Dr. Joseph F Coughlin. Dr. Coughlin is the founder and director of the Massachusetts Institute of Technology's aging lab. It is a multidisciplinary research program created to understand the behavior of the 50+ population, the role of technology in their lives, and the tremendous opportunity for innovation to improve the quality of life for older adults and their families.

After reading Dr. Coughlin's book and based on my experience in working with my caring and generous clients, I recognized that a bell curve not only represents the accumulation and distribution of financial assets but also depicts the unique gifts we all carry with us in our giving wheelhouse. As donors and aspiring philanthropists, we strive to do all we can for family and meaningful causes. We can do so with our satchel of wheelhouse gifts that we carry with us. So, let's take a closer look at our common life journey.

There are three stages to the curve relating to our life journey: #1 is accumulation, #2 is opportunity, and #3 is distribution. Let's take a deeper dive into the accumulation phase.

The Life Journey of Aspirational Giving

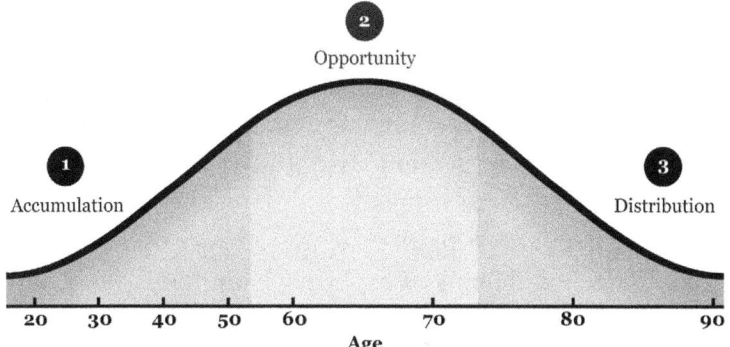

Accumulation is between birth and ends at approximately age 55, with an ending age that varies depending on an individual's life journey. Our life is centered on the development of self, family, and career during this accumulation phase. The focus is on obtaining a formal education, typically through the first 25 years of life. It is a time of learning and developing both platonic and love relationships. We learn about all those relationships and gain experience and wisdom from them. We gain experiences from our travel, family, and work — all through which we grow in maturity and life experience. We develop skills and talents during this accumulation on both a professional and personal level. It is during this accumulation phase when we discover and further develop our abilities and our talents. We also recognize the power of difference. By noting experiential differences as we age, we can zero in our interests and passions. Our experiences — both good and bad — result in finding what we like, what we don't like, and gaining the experience, maturity, and wisdom to discern the difference.

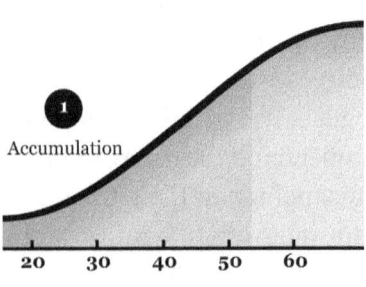

Let me use an example to illustrate the power of experiencing the difference. Let's say you graduate from college and work for a boss who has differences from how you were raised and your early life beliefs. With this first boss, you find out that there are some things that you like about their leadership or management style. But you also recognize that there are some things you do not like, so you consciously begin to recognize the importance of discerning the difference. Then you experience another boss in another job with a different personality. You once again recognize some things you like and some things you don't like. You accumulate numerous experiences in all facets of your life from your family, career, neighbors, travel, the world, and so on. As you experience many differences over time, you become much better, gaining life wisdom at understanding what you like and what you don't like and what is important and what is not.

There is more during this phase of accumulation. During this first phase of accumulation, it is also (hopefully!) a period of financial wealth accumulation. You have learned the importance of accumulating financial savings both for emergencies and for your later years. Over the years, you also develop financial values and attitudes from your life experience during this accumulation phase.

Also, during this period, you have learned some hard personal, life, and work-related chapters. There are times of ecstatic joy, stressful challenges, utter despair, and heart-wrenching disappointments. Your first role models and life guides are your parents and other adults, such as teachers and coaches. Some experiences you never want to repeat, some you would like to repeat, and some may reinforce an existing attitude or previous experience.

During this phase, you accumulate and develop three of the four wheelhouse gifts: talents, trust, and treasure. Treasure includes income, your financial savings, possibly business value, real estate, and other financial resources that contribute to a growing net worth. You are accumulating your relationships — your family, social, professional, and community. You are taught, mentored, and coached in life. You are life-learning. You accumulate and hopefully retain your trusted relationships. You may want to ensure trust. Close relationships don't wither away by being proactive in retaining contact with those close to you. Life is a give and take, and so are relationships!

I mentioned we are hopefully accumulating three of the four wheelhouse gifts. You notice I didn't mention time. During the accumulation phase, we have little free time. We are either spending our time or investing our time. For most of us, we invest our time during this phase by accumulating our other three gifts – talents, treasure, and trust. We invest our time to increase our income, earning potential, and financial wealth. We build our talents in the form of education and skillsets. We may be investing our time in building a professional practice, a business, or professional skills. And lastly, we are (hopefully) investing our time developing and cultivating trusted relationships with family, close friends, and within our profession and community.

With all this said, free time is minimal during accumulation. During this period, what free time we have is many times spent on personal recreation for maintaining physical, spiritual, mental, and emotional health! It is crucial to discern how you use your allotted time. Are you spending it wisely? Are you wasting time on frivolous items? Are you investing your time to accumulate the gifts for giving?

More Questions to Ponder

1. During the accumulation phase, how did you invest your time in accumulating talents, treasure, and trusted relationships?

2. In the years ahead, how might you better invest your time in building and retaining life-giving relationships with family and friends?

3. With limited time during the accumulation phase, did you feel "in balance" building trusted relationships, talents, and treasure?

CHAPTER 7

Key #3: Understand Your Life Journey

Phase 2 Opportunity

The life journey of aspirational giving consists of three phases: accumulation, opportunity, and distribution. In the previous chapter, we covered the accumulation phase. Now, let's look at the second phase: opportunity.

Opportunity is the age span between 55 and 75 years old. Dr. Coughlin highlights this concept of opportunity in his book on the longevity economy. Having served people who are retiring in this opportunity zone, I've come to recognize their common characteristics as they prepare for, transition into, or navigate "traditional retirement." At this point in life, in the opportunity phase, your wheelhouse should be chock-full of your accumulated trusted relationships, your talents and skillsets, and your accumulated treasure, which is typically reflected in your net worth. You are hopefully at the point in your life when you have flexibility and time freedom. Many of us relish and strive for time freedom. With time

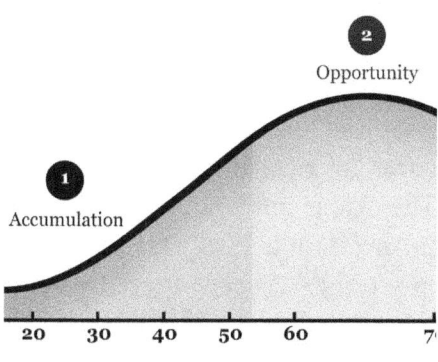

freedom, our traditional societal concept of retirement becomes an archaic term. I invite you to look up the definition of retirement and suggest that an alternative term, life transition, is much more descriptive.

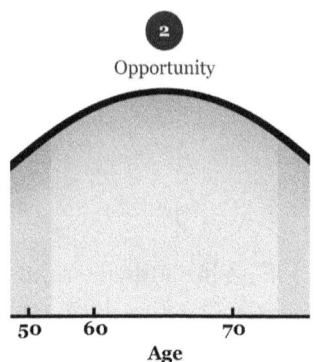

These days, with time freedom and the resulting lifestyle flexibility, we typically make life adjustments to transition from one life chapter to another. In this phase, we typically gain the freedom to use our time as we choose. We are in a transition, not retired, from life! It is often the time for a second career, a second act, or, for some, a third or even fourth act on this stage.

Many times, but not all, I have found the primary challenge in preparing for this life transition does not regard financial readiness. Many people may be financially secure, not rich by any means, but financially comfortable. The challenge then becomes one of transitioning into the unknown. What will I transition to? This realization can be unsettling. It is unchartered waters. They are not sure what their schedule is going to look like. During their working years with family and career, they may have had a very structured day and week.

I often shared with my clients that three things are needed as you transition during this period of opportunity. You need to have a purpose to your life and a purpose to your day — the reason to get up in the morning and look forward to that day. You have to structure your day. And the last thing that is needed in this transitional period of opportunity is social engagement — how will you socially engage with others?

As Dr. Coughlin shared, if we are fortunate enough to have longer, healthier lifespans, we have the opportunity for other pursuits. That's why this is called the opportunity phase. If you are fortunate enough to have good health, time freedom, flexibility, accumulated skills and talents, trusting relationships, and sufficient treasure for financial security, you recognize that this stage truly is a time of opportunity!

The opportunity phase is also the period of peak motivation time for giving. The peak motivation is derived from the research documented in the book *Gerotranscendence: A Developmental Theory* of Positive Aging by Dr. Lars Tornstam. Tornstam is a Swedish sociologist who explored a new theory in gerontology called gerotranscendence. In his well-documented research, his theory of gerotranscendence depicts our growing need to give as we age – it increases as we get older. It is typically in this opportunity phase that we have the greatest desire to give back, mentor the younger generation, and reflect on how we can make this world a better place. The theory reflects some overlooked developmental changes related to increased life satisfaction.

If you look at the opportunity phase in the overall context of our common life journey, we can align our inherent need to give with a defined purpose and passions. With our time, freedom, and flexibility, we have an excellent opportunity to make an impact! Suppose we can help people at this stage of life, no matter their life position or status, by awakening their giving spirit and unleashing their giving potential. In that case, we can leverage the power of each individual to transform and make significant impacts for positive, life-enhancing transformations. We can better the lives of others, improve the environment, and fundamentally "do more good!"

More Questions to Ponder

1. As you assess your own life journey, at what ages would you consider your own opportunity phase?
2. How might you leverage your accumulated gifts to support meaningful causes?
3. As you reflect on the opportunity phase of your life journey, do you think your purpose in life will change? How?

CHAPTER 8

Key #3: Understand Your Life Journey

Phase 3 Distribution

Thus far, we have learned about the accumulation and opportunity phases of the life journey of aspirational giving. Now, let's look at the third stage — the distribution phase. The age range in the distribution phase varies depending on your life journey.

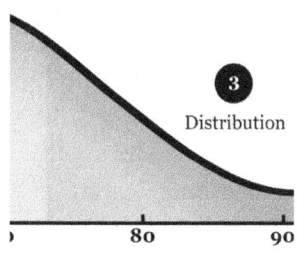

The age span is approximately from the early 70s until death — and its influences are felt long after in the lives of your family and the causes you champion.

This phase is a time for reflection on life's meaning. It is a time to review your life: was your life well-lived? Was it a life of significance? Did you make a difference? This distribution stage is when you ponder your legacies, including the perpetuation of personal and family values through your shared stories and lessons learned.

As a possible paradigm shift in thinking, may I suggest that spending your time during the distribution phase is a time to invest to ensure succeeding generations' success? This time investment may be with your children, grandchildren, and other family members as you share family activities, memories, and stories of chapters learned. It may be in youth sports or volunteering in the schools. In addition, your time during this distribution phase can be invested in organizing, documenting, and capturing personal and family values, memories, stories, and chapters learned through written or digital recording.

The distribution phase is a time of inquiry, spirituality, reflection, and action to recognize and perpetuate meaningful beliefs, values, and causes. It is a time for further refining and ensuring your intended financial legacy — how you pass on your financial assets.

The Essence of a More Life-Giving Perspective

I have found that there is a critical need to re-interpret the distribution conversation. Currently, the word estate is used in the typical phrases of estate planning, estate documents, estate settlement, estate attorney, and others as part of this time of life. As advocates for the positive, life-giving appreciation and celebration of individual lives of significance, I suggest that we purge the word "estate" from our vocabulary. Thus, moving forward, I have replaced the word estate and its negative connotation of darkness, death, and dying with the single word legacy to reflect a well-lived, significant, and impactful life.

Let's shift our attitude to one of leaving a personal legacy. Based on my 25 years of professional experience helping clients and their families, I found that many people in the opportunity or distribution phase associate the word estate with death and dying. It is a direct link to facing their mortality, and the implication for their families is not a pleasant thought. The word estate may be part of the routine language of attorneys, the media, and other professionals, but not for the individual that wants to feel their life was a life well-lived and had meaning and significance. Planning, living, and leaving a positive, caring, loving legacy is much more motivating and meaningful. It is about appreciating and celebrating you, your life, and all the goodness you bring to this world.

In that same vein, the shift in thinking transforms the perception from one's mortality to an attitude of appreciating and celebrating your life. The term legacy is uplifting. Legacy, legacy planning, legacy attorney, and legacy settlement convey a much more celebratory, positive impact that reflects the good we have done for family and causes. Legacy provides us with an aspiration to reach higher, to strive to make a difference, and impart transformations for good. As we become more effective donors, it is essential to adopt this attitudinal change, incorporate legacy in our language, and serve as an advocate for promoting legacy planning and all the goodness it conveys. This paradigm shift in outlook provides the motivation and perspective to engage more comfortably in conversations and an aspiration to give back and to make a difference.

We will all leave multiple legacies, both financial and non-financial. What you do, or don't do, will either be a positive or negative experience for your loved ones. In any case, legacies are created through the collaborative engagement of your inner and other circles of influence. It is essential to review your legacy plans to ensure your legacy-impacting legal documents are in place. Also, to supplement your legal documents, the distribution stage is the time to ensure that your more personal affairs are organized and your loved ones know your intentions and directions.

In summary, the life journey of aspirational giving is a journey of three distinct phases: an accumulation phase, an opportunity phase, and the distribution phase. In the accumulation phase, we are accumulating our talents, our trusted relationships, our treasure. We are thoughtful, caring stewards of our fourth gift – our precious time – to spend and invest wisely. We build trusted relationships and talents, earn an education, and increase our income and financial savings. Hopefully, our wheelhouse of gifts is full of our accumulated talents, treasure, and trust in the opportunity phase. We look forward to having the time, freedom, and flexibility to choose those activities that most appeal to us. It is also the time if we are fortunate to have good health, to give and do more. Lastly, there is the distribution phase, where we distribute our time, talents, treasure, and time in the form of shared stories, sharing of our talents, financial donations, and volunteering our time. We, mentor, set the example for and pass on pass on both our financial and non-financial legacies to children, grandchildren, and to our favorite causes.

More Questions to Ponder

1. How might you distribute your accumulated wisdom, memories, and values to succeeding generations?
2. Have you considered the positive, life-giving essence of focusing on "legacy" as a replacement term for the negative connotations of "estate"?
3. How might you distribute your financial assets to benefit both your family and your meaningful causes?

CHAPTER 9

Key #4: Engage in Meaningful Conversations

Up to this point, we've introduced our common donor roots, circles of influence, and three of the five keys: the use of inquiry to reveal, our giving wheelhouse, and our common life journey.

Now we are going to discuss Key #4 Engage in Meaningful Conversations. Nonprofits and professional advisors often refer to these types of conversations as philanthropic conversations. With this concept, we will be answering the following questions: What are meaningful conversations? Who are they with? What are the different types of conversations? How do we engage in these types of conversations?

What are meaningful conversations?

These conversations are deep, reflective conversations. They are typically private, personal, and positive. They are life-giving and uplifting. They bring meaning to your life. They are about family stories, values, passions, chapters learned, and beliefs. They reflect who you are and your purpose in life. They provide more profound answers to what is inspiring, exciting, and motivating to you.

Who are meaningful conversations with?

First, these conversations are with yourself during reflection, prayer, or other quiet times. As you may recall, Aspire is the avatar of your giving heart. You should always lead with your heart and follow your moral compass to your north star to serve family and those causes meaningful to you. To do this effectively takes regular personal time.

Second, you should also engage in meaningful conversations with your significant other (SO) in a timely, informal way. The SO serves as a great facilitator, partner, and sounding board for you.

Third, engaging a donor coach, taking a course, or reading a book like this is beneficial. Like any good coach, a donor coach can help you discover your strengths and what is meaningful to you. The donor coach sits next to you and guides you to follow the donor roadmap.

Fourth, meaningful conversations are also with nonprofit professionals. It is vital to align your strengths and passions (causes) and goals (purpose). This alignment, in turn, will lead to you engaging in thoughtful conversations with nonprofit and related-cause organizations. Fifth, you may also engage in meaningful conversations with professional advisors. These advisors, such as certified financial planners, certified public accountants, insurance professionals, and legacy planners, are trained and experienced with practical expertise in a specific niche.

What are the types of meaningful conversations?

There are conversations of your giving heart and conversations of your thinking head.

While you should always lead with your giving heart

and engage your significant other, these heart conversations are emotional and centered around family, passions, and your favorite causes. These heart conversations light up and clarify your moral compass to your north star. Conversations of the heart are the counseling types of conversations existing in faith traditions and spirituality. They reflect your soul, spirit, and core being.

Conversations of the thinking head deal with options, pros and cons, and what makes rational, practical, and down-to-earth sense. They are about data, numbers, and timing. Thinking head conversations are about paperwork and the practical, rational aspects of

getting things done and implementing your giving strategy to achieve your goals. These conversations typically reside in the world of professional advisors like accountants, lawyers, insurance, and financial professionals. A donor coach can help facilitate the heart and head conversations because they are trained, experienced, and comfortable in these conversational areas.

Engaging in meaningful conversations is essential to recognize that they are vital to becoming an effective donor. Your success in these conversations will enable you to understand, clarify, design your giving plan, and achieve your giving goals. One proven way to engage in these conversations is to keep these conversations casual and straightforward. It is much easier to introduce and talk about meaningful topics with intentional, positive, appreciative, open-ended questions. Always take time to listen and learn. It is helpful to write down questions or jot down specific topics when they come to mind so that, when the opportunity arises, the topic may be introduced with selected members of your inner circle before they are introduced to nonprofit professionals, counselors, or professional advisors.

In this chapter, we learned that meaningful conversations are also called philanthropic conversations. They are highly personal conversations within ourselves and our circles of influence. Engage in these conversations and apply positive, appreciating questions to listen, clarify, and understand.

How do you engage in meaningful conversations?

As in many areas of life, if we know the right questions to ask, we can discover, learn, and make more effective decisions. Engaging in meaningful conversations can be difficult both from an emotional perspective and in knowing what questions to ask! As shared in a previous section, donor-outlook questions (DOQ) serve as the fuel that drives conversations. Whether it be every-day conversations or engaging in philanthropic, meaningful conversations, questions direct the conversations. Donor-outlook questions help you engage in meaningful conversations with family members, professional advisors, and nonprofit professionals. With the confidence and know-how of engaging others, we bridge a communications void that restrains human engagement in meaningful conversations.

More Questions to Ponder

1. When was the last time you engaged in a meaningful conversation with your significant other? Your children? Your parents?

2. Have you recently engaged in a meaningful conversation with any of your professional advisors? If so, whom? Who initiated the conversation?

3. As you recall your most recent meaningful conversations, were they conversations of the heart or conversations of the head?

CHAPTER 10

Key #5: Follow the Donor's Roadmap

So far, we've introduced shared roots of our giving heart, discussed circles of influence, and the first four keys: inquire to learn, our wheelhouse, our life journey, and meaningful conversations.

Key #5 is Follow the Donor's Roadmap. The appreciative donor learning process is just that — a process or roadmap that you will follow to discover, align, design, and implement a strategy for giving. Since we are traveling on Philanthropy Way to somewhere new on this giving journey, you must have a road map (or GPS) to get to your destination. You need your destination and then to have

milestones to assess and navigate successfully. This truth is vital in many aspects of life, whether planning a roadtrip vacation, manufacturing a product, or preparing for a major life transition, such as traditional retirement. People aspire to better their families, communities, or meaningful causes. People want to have a destination, a roadmap, and guides to show them the way. They want to be fluent in the language, learn their route options, and how to best navigate to their destination, whatever that may be.

The same is true for anyone that wants to become a better, smarter, more effective donor. Most donors would like to become better and make a difference. Up to now, there has been very little help in the form of a step-by-step process or learning roadmap to help individual donors travel their Philanthropy Way to become more informed and learn how to make wiser, more beneficial giving decisions. This roadmap serves as the process for donors to become better versions of themselves and be more effective in their giving to their families and those meaningful causes.

The Origin of the Appreciative Donor Learning Process

In my search for a donor-outlook process, I searched high and low for a donor roadmap that originated from the viewpoint or perspective of the individual donor. I first reviewed the financial planning process published by the Certified Financial Planner® (CFP) Board of Standards. The CFP process, while excellent for financial planning, does not, and should not, address the emotional foundations of giving. With some additional research, I discovered the Appreciative Inquiry (AI) process. As an extended descendent of the Socratic method of asking questions, the AI process engages individuals and groups in self-determined change. It revolutionized organizational development and was a precursor to the rise of positive organizational studies and the strength-based movement. It was developed at the Weatherford School of Management at Case Western Reserve University in the 1980s. At that time, the emphasis on problem-solving was limited by any kind of improvement in the individual (such as social improvement), so researchers at Case Western created new models of inquiry to focus on the strengths of individuals, groups, diversity, and perspective. The AI process is a life-giving, strengths-based approach that helps people focus on their unique strengths and do well. So, it focuses on how one's talents and energy can be a channel for good and, therefore, the greater good for family and groups, causes, or passions. The keyword is personal strengths, with the ultimate goal being to improve upon and leverage your existing strengths, your gifts in your wheelhouse.

By applying philanthropic inquiry (PI) with a donor's perspective, I extracted the best from the appreciative inquiry process and my professional experience. I elicited a donor-outlook learning process tailored to serve as a roadmap for donors to become wiser, fluent, and more effective with their giving. I named this process the Appreciative Donor Learning Process (ADLP). A general graphic of the learning process is shown on the next page.

This comprehensive and integrated process embeds and leverages the emotional motivations of philanthropy – the giving heart – to answer the fundamental question of "Why give?" It also engages the rational thinking head in the decision-making. It lifts and magnifies the life-giving motivations of donors to pursue their aspirations, passions, and purpose to benefit both family and causes. With the defined goal of aligning purpose, passion, and personal strengths (shown in the middle of the above diagram), this

five-step process provides a complete roadmap that nicely integrates both the giving heart and thinking head needs and addresses the donor's inherent aspiration to give to their families and their causes.

The Learning Process

In sequence, the roadmap consists of 5 steps or milestones: Discovery, Dream, Design, Delivery, and Destiny. Let's take a closer look at each of these five steps.

Step 1 is discovery. In the discovery stage, we ask the question, "Why do I give?" We intentionally clarify and align our passions and what we enjoy doing with our strengths (our gifts for giving) to find our sweet spot. In this step, we answer Who do I give to? and where do I give?

Step 2 is dream. We all have hopes and dreams. You dream about what you would improve, what you would like to become, and what you would like to make better – your vision for the future. The dream step provides the answers to both the broad categorical and specific organizational Who? question and Where?

Step 3 is design. In the design step, you design your giving plan to both family and outreach. During this step, you affirm answers to your heart-dominant questions: why do I give? who do I give to? and where do I give? You then assess how they affect your design. You then address the thinking head questions of How do I give? What do I give? When do I give? How much do I give? With your newly acquired donor-outlook knowledge, use DOQ to explore possibilities and options with advisors. With your confidant at your side, depending on your advisory circle, you seek guidance from nonprofit professionals, professional advisors, and possibly a philanthropy coach to answer these thinking head questions to help design your plan.

Step 4 is delivery. With your blueprint in hand, we then move to delivery (the action items needed to implement your philanthropic strategy). You will depend heavily on your advisory circle at this step to implement and deliver. DOQ was your primary tool in the design step, but you will continue key conversations throughout the delivery stage. Delivery includes meaningful conversations with your inner circle, nonprofit professionals and professional advisors such as CPAs, CAP®s, CFP®s, legacy attorneys, insurance agents, or financial advisors. It should also include additional conversations and decisions to address family dynamics, intentions, and related challenges. These conversations include reviewing and executing your legal documents and structures (wills, power of attorney, trust documents) and other non-legal family love letters and letters of intent, as well as other action items such as recording family memories and family history.

Step 5 is destiny. During this last step, we reassess, review, and resolve residual items from our implemented plan. In this step, you review and create your living and lasting legacies, both non-financial and financial, for your family, meaningful nonprofits, and other causes. Periodically step back and look at the overall strategy in its broader context. This review should be completed annually in your personal reflection and every three years with a more in-depth review. The following are some questions to ask: Are we achieving our intended goals? Are we transforming our purpose-driven life of success into a lasting life of significance? Will my children, grandchildren, and succeeding generations be better off because of my life, and will my causes be advanced? Hopefully, all our legacies reflect a purpose-driven life well lived! Your financial legacy includes how things are structured and implemented financially. Your non-financial legacy includes documenting, organizing, and perpetuating values, beliefs, memories, chapters learned, family history, and dedication to causes that are passed on to children, grandchildren, and succeeding generations.

To sum it up, the Appreciative Donor Learning Process is your roadmap for your giving journey. You can transform your purpose-driven life from a well-lived life of success to a life of meaningful, impactful, and lasting significance.

More Questions to Ponder

1. What kind of questions (Key #1) would be important to you in each of the five (5) steps of the process?

2. How might engaging in meaningful conversations (Key #4) help you navigate this roadmap?

3. In reflecting on your wheelhouse gifts (Key #2) and your life journey (Key #3), what steps of the learning process are most important to you?

Part III. Leverage the 5 Keys for a Brighter Future

This section summarizes the book and gives information on the complete Aspirational Philanthropist Learning Series.℠

CHAPTER 11

Recap the Basics

Throughout this book, you have learned to:

1. Recognize that you are a philanthropist. You give to your family, community, and causes.
2. Tap your roots as a donor. It is in our DNA to give.
3. Engage your circles of influence (inner, advisory, learning, and beneficiary circles).
4. Embrace donor-outlook philanthropy to engage in meaningful conversations with donor outlook questioning.

The five keys help us take the conversation and practically carry it out.

Key #1 Inquire to Learn. Narrowing our inquiry to philanthropy with a donor-outlook perspective gives us donor-outlook questioning (DOQ). DOQ is a derivative of the Socratic method from a donor perspective, a positive, life-giving appreciative approach for the donor to ask intentional questions. The DOQ method asks seven essential questions for framing and structuring the giving process.

Key #2 Appreciate Your Wheelhouse Gifts. There are four gifts: time, talent, treasure, and trust. Based on our own unique life experiences, we each have varying amounts of each of the four gifts. If we blend an individual's unique gifts in an appreciative, positive way to a common goal or purpose, the sum of the output is greater than the individual strengths.

Key #3 Understand Your Life Journey. There are three phases to our life journey: accumulation, opportunity, and distribution. Accumulation is the stage of life when we accumulate our talents, treasure, and trusted connections. Time is limited because we invest in gathering talents and skills, accumulating financial resources, and building relationships. Opportunity is when our wheelhouse is full of accumulated talents, experiences, financial assets, and trusted ties. Typically, it is during the opportunity that we have time freedom which provides us scheduling flexibility.

Distribution is a great time to invest in the succeeding generations, teach and share our accumulated wisdom, and capture memories that reflect our values. It is a time to firm up our non-financial legacy, perpetuate personal and family values, and record family history.

Key #4 Engage in Meaningful Conversations. We use donor-outlook questioning (DOQ) in a positive, appreciative way to engage and explore possibilities, learn and understand other's stories and perspectives, seek knowledge and answers and build relationships. We engage in meaningful conversations, both of the heart and the head, with our four circles of influence.

Key #5 Follow the Donor's Roadmap (the appreciative donor learning process). The DOQ method of asking seven questions helps us stay on track as we navigate our way through the five-step process. We define and target our purpose by aligning our passions, personal strengths, and the meaning and joy that it brings. This donor fundamentals book serves as the foundation for this approach.

Thank you for reading this book! I hope it was beneficial to you and that what you learned from this book serves as a springboard for your continued growth as an aspiring philanthropist.

Let's Do Some Good!
Greg

The Aspirational Philanthropist Learning Series[SM]

The Aspirational Philanthropist Learning Series[SM] is the first-of-its-kind series designed to guide donors using a roadmap as they seek to solidify their legacy through giving, both to their families and the causes that are important to them.

The step-by-step roadmap is presented through four courses, with each building on knowledge to enable individual donors to find how they can be the best stewards of their personal and financial resources as they seek to do good for their families, in their communities, and around the world.

This program equips donors with the knowledge, tools, and resources to take care of their families and to give wisely. With a mix of short, engaging narrated videos, tailored journal sheets, short self-quizzes to benchmark learning, and an annotated bibliography and references, donors will learn how to gain more meaning and impact.

Fundamentals, Discovery, Design, and Legacy

1. The **Fundamentals** course is the introductory course of the learning series and serves as an exploratory introduction. In this course, you will learn to embrace

your role as an aspiring philanthropist and learn about engaging your circles of influence. You will be treated to the five keys to effective donor giving. These five keys serve as the foundation for donors. From this course, you will get a taste of content in the remaining courses and can decide whether it is right for you to take more courses.

2. In the **Discovery** course, you will clarify your purpose and tap your donor roots to discover your passions and how you can meet your giving goals. You will align these passions and personal strengths with your purpose. In Discovery, you will also learn how to find and vet (perform the necessary due diligence) the organizations that will benefit from your generosity. You will learn what to look for and how best to research nonprofits and beneficiaries with a checklist that assures a thorough assessment of the organizations you are considering to support.

3. In the **Design** course, you will create your own integrated and comprehensive philanthropic plan that will benefit both your family and meaningful causes. With an emphasis on ensuring a tailored approach, you will learn financial tools, such as qualified charitable distributions (gifting from IRA assets), donor advised funds, charitable foundations and trusts, giving circles, charitable annuities, hometown impact investing, how to leverage technology, and leading-edge financial tools and techniques. You will also learn how and when to use these tools and what types of assets are the best to give, and when is best to give them.

4. In the **Legacy** course, you will learn to embrace a different outlook on legacy planning. You will learn how to create your legacies, financial and non-financial, for your family and favorite causes. You will recognize and embrace the newfound skill of engaging in meaningful conversations as a way of creating and perpetuating both your living

and lasting legacies. You will also learn how to enlist others in crafting your legacies through the documents, family love letters, and other tools and resources.

Now, let's do some good!
Greg

Part IV. Donor-Outlook Enrichment Readings

Consider each of the supplemental readings to Donor Fundamentals as key articles to provide enriched content that capture the essence of donor-outlook philanthropy. I hope they will complement and expand the knowledge you have obtained and inspire you to learn more.

Please add to your knowledge base as well by visiting my blog: *https://www.aspiretogive.com/resources/blog*

Enrichment Reading A

Advancing Philanthropy Through the Eyes & Heart of the Donor

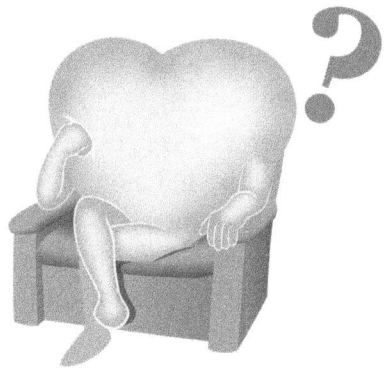

When you face a challenge at home, in your career, or in life, do you leverage the power of questions to discover, learn, and reveal possibilities? Do you evaluate how to move forward? With well-structured, specific questions serving as a means of inquiry, we discover the unknown so that we can make smart, more effective choices in our lives.

The motivation for this blog came from an audio book I listened to while on my daily walk. The author sparked me to question the typical philanthropic perspective. I realized that questions were the roots of Aspire to Give, the creation of the Appreciative Donor Learning Process, and of "donor-outlook philanthropy". As shared in a previous blog, the Appreciative Donor Learning Process serves as the roadmap for individuals to learn to become better donors to both their families and meaningful causes.

Let me explain what I mean by donor-outlook philanthropy. When I refer to donor-outlook, I am referencing the perspective of the individual donor. What are the aspirational hopes and dreams as viewed through the eyes and the heart of the donor or aspiring philanthropist? ... And, what might a donor do to achieve these hopes and dreams – their goals?

The book I listened to is titled *A More Beautiful Question: The Power of Inquiry to Spark Breakthrough Ideas* by Warren Berger. In his book, Mr. Berger documents, in great detail, his research on how the use of intentional, well-structured questions has been used throughout history to advance humankind. With numerous recent examples of Steve Jobs, Apple, Airbnb, Nike, Netflix, and more, he methodically proves that the source of all innovation is inquiry – asking questions.

What does this have to do with philanthropy and, specifically, the individual and donor-outlook philanthropy? Let me explain.

In his book, Mr. Berger shares the very simple concept: <u>Questions</u> + <u>Action</u> = <u>Innovation</u>; or, more simply, Q+A=I.

But wait! If you look at the original concept of Q + A = I, this formula seems to be lacking a goal for the innovation - there is a suppressed premise! For the individual, the goal represents the dreams and hopes of the donor. These dreams, hopes, and aspirations reflect a vision ("V") that we all spiritually hold in one form or another for ourselves, our families, and our causes.

Now, let's apply this formula to the individual donor as a means to advance philanthropy. How might we innovate and unleash the inherent potential of donors to learn to become better givers to their families and meaningful causes?

If we say (1) inquiry is questioning and (2) it is the donor asking the questions, then we have a new concept from the viewpoint of the donor: Donor Outlook Questioning or "DOQ". It is the donor asking questions on how to achieve their hopes and dreams that is manifested in their goals.

Now, let's look more closely at the "A" (acting) part of Berger's original concept (Q+A=I). Who is doing the acting - the "doing", or "making things happen"?

It is the individual donor, of course! Each of us has hopes and dreams for the future, for our family, our community, and the world. We each have an inherent desire to reach out to "do good". So, in this simple equation, the "A" becomes the actions of the individual donor. Now what do we have? The original concept of Q+A=I now becomes: (DOQ) +A +V= I. Condensed to simple wording, the donor focuses on asking intentional, well-structured questions from their perspective on how to act (do) to achieve their vision (goals). Berger's original concept of Q + A = I has been adapted to the field of philanthropy and more specifically, tailored to individual "donor-outlook philanthropy" that is powered by donor-outlook questioning (DOQ).

Let's look at the source of philanthropic social innovation to advance philanthropy. The innovation is a paradigm shift to view from the donor's perspective. All we need now are donors schooled with the knowledge, tools, and questioning techniques! With a proven learning roadmap in hand, the donor is now motivated and empowered to do more for their family and philanthropic causes.

There you have it! We tailored Berger's simple proven recipe of Q + A = I into donor-outlook philanthropy that is fueled with questions. What is critical in this process is to provide and tailor the learning program to the donor - to the aspiring philanthropist. This learning program teaches the donor how to tap and leverage their personal strengths to do more good for their family and outreach.

ENRICHMENT READING B

Why Do You Get up in the Morning?

As basic as this question may seem, there is a much deeper meaning. What is your purpose for living? What makes you want to get out of the bed in the morning?

We fall into a daily routine, If we give thought to why we get up in the morning, it is a time of personal reflection or spiritual engagement.

Let me propose to you that our purpose for living is to learn, to light, and to love. To clarify, in a previous blog I referred to the life journey of aspirational giving. It's divided into different phases: accumulation, opportunity, and distribution. A corollary of this life journey of aspirational giving is the life journey of aspirational learning, lighting, and loving.

Live to Learn

As noted previously, the early stages of our life journey is when we live to learn. We learn from our parents. We learn how to walk and become independent. Hopefully as we grow, we learn to be responsible and accountable for our choices.

We learn from our formal education in school and college as well as career-related education. We learn from our teachers, from mentors, from athletic coaches, from our friends' parents and from those who influence us. We have lived to learn.

Live to Light

Then comes a time in this life journey of aspirational giving where we began to learn to light. We continue to learn ourselves. Lessons learned from the school of hard knocks and different trials and tribulations. But there comes a time we live to learn and to light.

What do I mean "to light"? When we live to light it means we are teaching others by setting an example. We are lighting the pathway for our children. We guide, teach, and coach those we lead. When done in the appreciative, positive way, it allows those we lead in light to become better versions of themselves. This is most notable if you are a parent, grandparent, teacher, mentor or in any teaching role. You become the light that enables others to live their life in a positive, giving way. We become the teacher not the student when we live in the light.

Live to Love

During this whole journey of aspirational giving, hopefully, we have learned to love. Most typically this is reflected in loving parents. Parents who bestow love upon us, and as we live, they've shown us how to love.

Through the love demonstrated by our teachers, coaches, mentors, and others we have learned to love. From their examples of giving, we have learned to love and we have learned how to light.

In summary, the life journey of aspirational giving also embodies the principles of living to learn, to light, and to love. Our purpose for getting up in the morning is to learn through our life journey. It is also to light, to lead, and teach others so they too can live to learn, light, and love.

Lastly, we live to learn and to light in the common theme of love. To love life and to make an impact on the lives of others is the end goal.

So, why do you get out of bed in the morning? The answer may be as simple as, "I get out of the bed in the morning to learn, to light, and to love!"

Now, let's do some good!
Greg

ENRICHMENT READING C:

The 5 Pillars of Hometown Philanthropy

For many of us, our local community—our hometown—is where our heart is. We love our hometown! We want to see all of our community neighbors prosper, feel good, and go beyond surviving to thrive. But it is a struggle. Almost all hometowns have their challenges, whether those be housing, jobs, environmental issues, or the myriad number of other human needs that some face.

The key question we have all wrestled with at some point is how can we make our community better? What can we do as an individual, a family, and a business to enlist and leverage our strengths to make our hometowns better?

It is time for a paradigm shift in thinking. Once again, we need to approach our hometown challenges a little differently, which is a concept that will be explored in future blogs.

As a start, let me share with you the five local pillars of hometown philanthropy. They are:

- Citizens (Individuals)
- Foundations
- Nonprofits
- Government
- Businesses

Citizens: Everyone has an inherent desire to give to something greater than self. It is in our DNA. No matter what our background is, we have both inherent and accumulated gifts to give to causes greater than self. In most cases, people recognize their emotional need to help others, yet they may feel they are giving on their own without the benefit of sound guidance. Many individuals "wing-it" with their giving; donating generously to feel good but yet unsure if they are giving in a smart, impactful way. Individual donors may wonder who they should give to, how much to give, and how best to give. Oftentimes, individual donors are confused and would like a little help to understand how to give meaningfully to make a greater impact.

Foundations: In most cases, the premier foundation in most any hometown is the local Community Foundation. According to the Council on Foundations, there are more than 750 community foundations in both rural and urban communities in the United States. These community foundations serve as the central hub and resource for local philanthropy. In addition to local community foundations, oftentimes there are other types of foundation support. These can include either private family foundations that are tied to the local community or grant funding provided by bigger, regional or national foundations that are designated for the local community.

Nonprofits: In many cases, local nonprofits are started, funded, and championed by local individuals who have a passion for a specific cause. In some cases, such as the Boys and Girls Clubs, they are local branches of national organizations that serve a specific need. In most cases, the number one challenge for local nonprofits is funding. They can be funded by grants or revenues generated from events and sponsorships. Also included in this nonprofit category are churches, social groups such as local women's groups, and others that engage in community outreach. In many cases, these nonprofits and groups have their own community outreach activities and may reach out to others in the local community for additional resourcing and collaboration.

Government: Many people do not think of the local government as a "pillar" of philanthropy, but they are. Local government oftentimes does not recognize their own philanthropic role and importance as a pillar for hometown philanthropy. This change in government thinking is a needed paradigm shift to advance local community philanthropy. The local government agencies can be more pro-active to advance effective community development philanthropy. In later blogs, I will share ideas and specific steps on how local government can be more effective in community development philanthropy through collaborative partnering with the other pillars of hometown philanthropy.

Businesses: For many communities, local businesses serve as a key pillar for local philanthropy. They often provide support to nonprofits within the communities in the form of sponsorships, in-kind donations, and employee support. Business community outreach is well-intentioned to better the community and serves as goodwill marketing. But local businesses can do more and be more effective in filling their role for community development philanthropy. Again, this notion of how local businesses can be much more effective and be smarter with community outreach will be discussed more in-depth in future blogs as well.

So, now you have an understanding of the five pillars of hometown philanthropy. Each pillar strives to meet its own mission and "do good" within the community. However, in many cases, these pillars operate independently as "silos;" with a laser-focus on their specific mission.

Now, let's do some good!
Greg

Enrichment Reading D:

The 7 Essential Questions for Smart Giving

You have come to that point in your life when you realize that giving to others or to a cause greater than yourself is becoming more important and meaningful to you. You realize that your giving will bring meaning and purpose to your life and it will make you happier. And you also find it liberating and exhilarating to realize you are on the precipice of an uncharted cliff—and what you do next is up to you!

Many individuals would like to learn more about giving of themselves and their resources whether that is giving to their family, charities, or by giving in ways that they may not even know about. They aren't quite sure where to begin. They want to be smarter with their generosity and ensure what they are giving—be it time, talent, treasure, or trust—has the greatest impact possible on the causes that are important to them.

Realizing your desire to do more for others, embracing your giving heart and listening to your practical head are the means to an end when it comes to bringing giving to fruition. To begin the process, a certain amount of self-reflection will be required. Aristotle may have said it best with the following:

> *"To give away money is an easy matter and in any man's power. But to decide to whom to give it and how large and when, and for what purpose, is neither in every man's power nor an easy matter."*
>
> —Aristotle 360 B.C.

In considering your own situation, listed below are seven questions to think about and perhaps discuss in collaboration with a philanthropy coach as you nurture your growing desire to do more and aspire to learn the ways, tools, and techniques of giving. At Aspire to Give, we apply these seven essential questions in our proprietary process as part of the philanthropic conversation.

Why Give?

So much in life circles back to the fundamental question of "why?" In the end, the answer to the question "why," is our motivation—our reason—for doing something and when it comes to our giving—whether that be to family, to charity, or through social impact investing—each giver has a personal reason fueling the need to give.

Often it takes conversation and reflection to figure out your "why give" answer. In some cases, it may be the desire to make a difference, to "give back," to lend a helping hand to those in need, or to perpetuate personal and family values. In other cases, it could be your life was affected by a certain situation or event and you want to help others going through similar experiences.

Understanding and articulating your "why give" is the emotional connection and motivation for giving. It's the first and most important step to smart giving and the answer serves as the springboard in addressing the other six questions.

Who to Give to?

This is a question that is in direct correlation with your answer to "why give?" What is important with this question is to assure that your answers to the "why" and the "who" are intentionally aligned to be emotionally satisfying, meaningful, and mutually beneficial for all involved.

If your motivation for giving stems from a specific personal experience, the "who" might be a certain organization or passion that addresses what is important to you. If you want to give back simply because you can afford to do so, the answer of who to give to may be more complicated. In this instance, this will require some personal reflection followed by research.

As a good steward of your resources, you want to identify and screen the nonprofits that receive your gifts. What are your personal and family mission and the anticipated social return on investment (SROI) of your financial giving? What do you know about the nonprofit's board leadership, infrastructure, and composition? How much of your financial gift is used for social impact vs. organizational overhead? These are just a few of the questions to consider as you make your giving plan.

Where to Give?

Before deciding where to give, ask questions. Do the leg work required to ensure that the answer to where you give brings about your desired result and maximum impact.

Do you want to give within your local community? Or do you prefer to give regionally, nationally, or even overseas? If you give locally, is the nonprofit a local nonprofit or a community branch of a national nonprofit? If you give to a local branch, how much stays local and how much goes to the national affiliation?

When to Give?

Oftentimes, the bequest at death is the by-default option for when to give. There are other options such as "giving while living," which provides more control on directed giving and gives you the joy of seeing your generosity used during your lifetime. Another option for when to give may be anticipating the sale of real estate or a business. Sometimes, tax consequences may be a factor for considering the timing of your giving.

If you are giving your time and talents to a specific cause or organization, when to get involved may depend on your family situation, your health, and your availability. Are you retired, still working but have flexibility within your schedule, or is your time limited to weekends only? Is this something you will do on your own or will you invite your children or grandchildren to participate and use it as a teaching moment instilling the values that matter to you?

What to Give?

For some, the choice is simple. For others with higher incomes or net worth, what to give becomes more challenging. Cash, securities, real estate, closely held business stock, life insurance, retirement assets, or even collectibles can be given. Each giver should assess their situation to determine what makes the most sense to give.

It's also a good time to broaden your horizons and think beyond money or material gifts. Maybe when you begin your giving journey, the first step is to offer your time. Getting involved in a local charity or church organization that is doing work that is close to your heart may be a good option as you consider what to give in the long-term. Think about your specific talents and check within your community to see if you could contribute in a different way that is just as valuable as a monetary donation—perhaps more so through the relationships that will be established through volunteering.

How to Give?

Again, expanding your typical understanding of giving is a good place to start. Is it best for you to start out by offering your time and talents or making a financial gift? Would it benefit your hometown more to start with a combination of these? Should you give directly, or through some other means such as a donor advised fund, private foundation, charitable gift annuity, or a specific type of charitable trust? What is the tax impact? Should you give as an incentive, as an impact investment, or to facilitate community development? Do you want to engage your children or grandchildren in your giving?

How to give is a layered question with answers coming in many forms. There is not a cookie-cutter answer that can be applied to all. That is why working with a trusted, professional advisor may help provide a clear sense and understanding of how you give impacts the overall giving aspirations you have defined for yourself.

How Much to Give?

This may be one of the more complex and difficult questions to answers as many factors come into play. It is common for individuals who want to give to ask: How much can I give and still ensure my family's financial security and personal financial independence? If you have enough money for your own lifetime and for your family's financial security, you may be able to experience the joys of "giving while living" or, if you prefer, leaving donations as a bequest at death. At this point, consulting with a trusted advisor may be a good way to determine exactly what can be allocated for personal needs, family obligations, and the greater good.

Your Next Step

There you have it—the seven essential questions for smart giving. Our hope is that these questions help raise your awareness on the process behind giving. For it is through the giving of ourselves and our resources, including financial resources, that we can make a difference, give back, and help those in need. It is through intentional and aligned giving that we can feel really good while finding a true sense of purpose and meaning in our lives.

When you think about it, intentional, meaningful, and impactful giving is not that easy. It requires some soul-searching thought of who we are, our values, and what is really important to us. We have what we refer to as our giving wheelhouse—our time, our talents, our treasures (financial resources), and our trusted relationships (personal network)—all available as giving means. We have choices to make as to where we give—our family, charity, a special cause, or social impact investing within our communities. We integrate the seven essential questions within the giving process to discover and align our purpose with our passion, design our giving plan, and then deliver our own unique giving gifts. Using our philanthropic giving process, we can then give in a way that is smart, effective and impactful to create both a lasting and a living legacy for ourselves and our families.

Our hope—our aspiration—is that we may serve you, those with a "giving heart," and equip you with the resources and knowledge to become an even better version of your giving self. Aspire to Give® will continue to share with you our leading-edge thinking through our blogs, articles, books, and other resources. In fact, a more in-depth look at these seven essential questions is explored in my new book, *Aspire to Give® How to Create a More Meaningful Life through Your Giving*, is now available as both a digital Kindle book and a print-on-demand version may be purchased at amazon.com.

We want you to consider Aspire to Give as your personal resource and as a trusted source to help you become the best you can be on your life's journey of aspirational giving!

Let's do some good!
Greg

Also by Greg Doepke

Aspire to Give®:
How to Create a More Meaningful Life Through Your Giving

Available on Amazon

www.ingramcontent.com/pod-product-compliance
Lightning Source LLC
Chambersburg PA
CBHW070114230526
45472CB00004B/1253